ABOUT DINOSAURS

By Margery Morris

Colour illustrations by
Michael Spink

Penguin Books

Penguin Books Ltd, Harmondsworth, Middlesex, England
Penguin Books Inc., 7110 Ambassador Road, Baltimore, Maryland 21207, U.S.A.
Penguin Books Australia Ltd, Ringwood, Victoria, Australia

First published 1972

Made and printed in Great Britain by Alabaster Passmore & Sons Ltd, London and Maidstone

Table of Contents

This book is for
ROBERT JOHN SANSOME

2. INTO THE JURASSIC

3. INTO THE CRETACEOUS

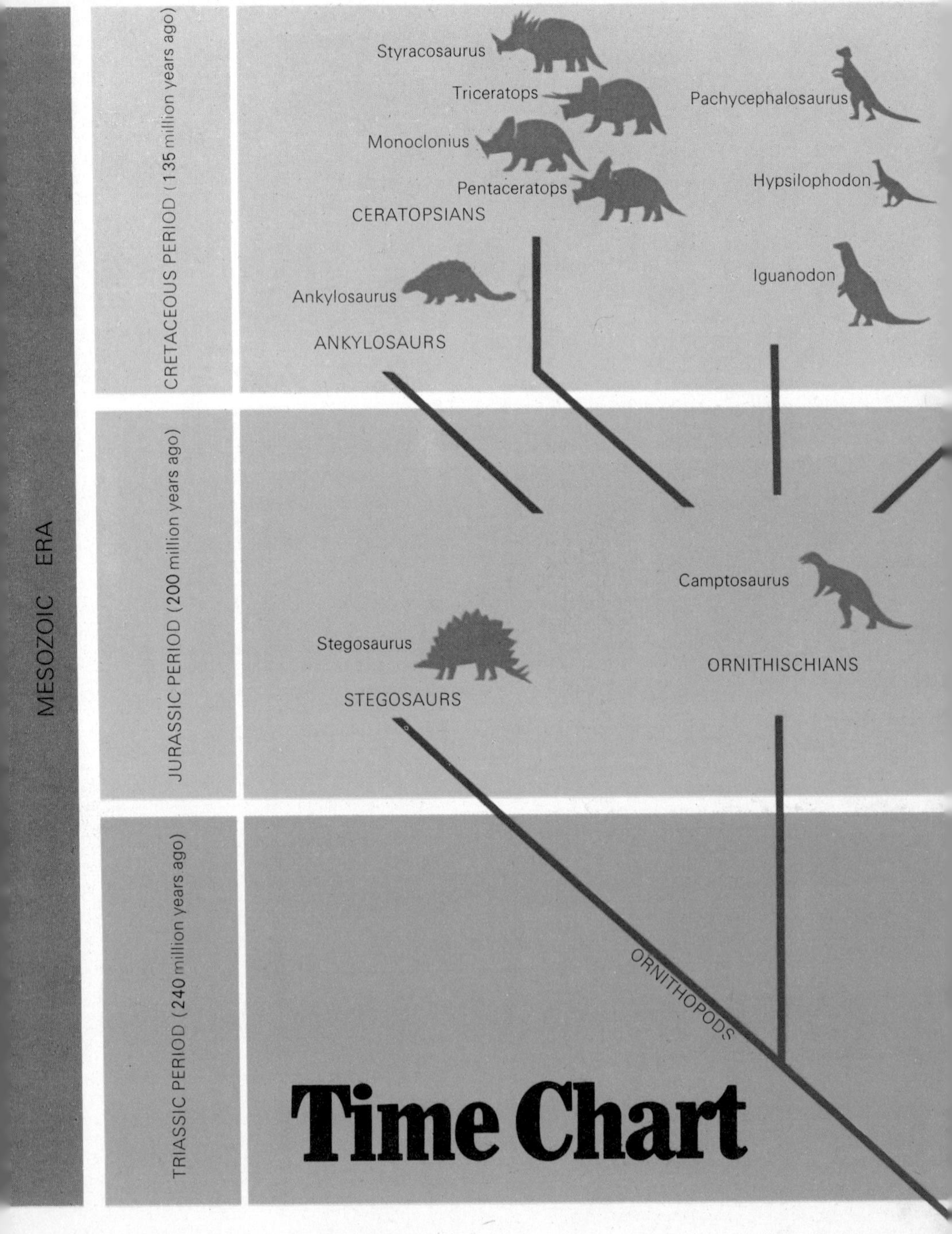

Time Chart

MESOZOIC ERA

CRETACEOUS PERIOD (135 million years ago)

Styracosaurus

Triceratops

Monoclonius

Pentaceratops

CERATOPSIANS

Pachycephalosaurus

Hypsilophodon

Iguanodon

Ankylosaurus

ANKYLOSAURS

JURASSIC PERIOD (200 million years ago)

Camptosaurus

Stegosaurus

STEGOSAURS

ORNITHISCHIANS

TRIASSIC PERIOD (240 million years ago)

ORNITHOPODS

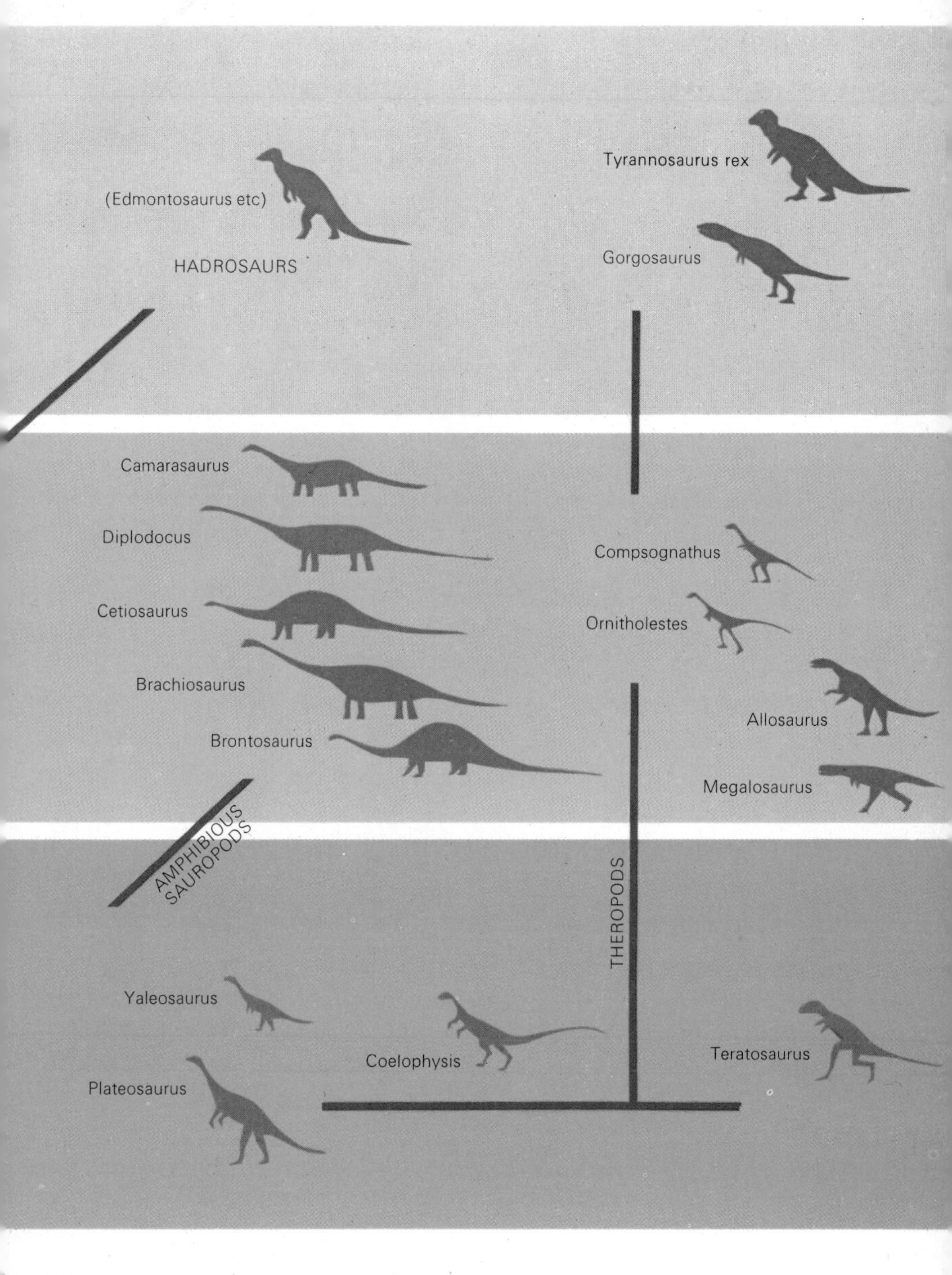
Tyrannosaurus rex
(Edmontosaurus etc)
HADROSAURS
Gorgosaurus
Camarasaurus
Diplodocus
Compsognathus
Cetiosaurus
Ornitholestes
Brachiosaurus
Allosaurus
Brontosaurus
Megalosaurus
AMPHIBIOUS SAUROPODS
THEROPODS
Yaleosaurus
Coelophysis
Teratosaurus
Plateosaurus

Ancestors

ABOUT DINOSAURS
MORE ABOUT DINOSAURS

Quizkid daring traveller, brave hunter, single-minded scientist, prepares for a safari into Time Past. His perilous quest – the long-dead mighty dinosaurs.

Into the Triassic

Two hundred and forty million years in the past, the dawn of a Triassic day. No birdsong greets it. Nothing moves in this primitive landscape but water and clouds, and the wind in the reeds.

Almost hidden but wide awake, two PHYTOSAURS lurk near the unsuspecting traveller from the future.

What tracks are these? Careless of danger, Quizkid takes up the trail . . .
Not a dinosaur but a mammal-like reptile, CYNOGNATHUS – 'dog-face'.

EUPELOR is a giant amphibian.
He eats fish. Perhaps he also eats mammals.
This animal met its death when it came to drink at the stream. Quizkid's quick eye notes the pelvic bones and the teeth. He identifies it as a dinosaur, COELOPHYSIS.

'Phytosaur' means 'plant reptile', but those teeth were not designed for eating plants.

Cynognathus is awake and hunting. One snap of those dog-type teeth . . . Quizkid had better take care.

Mammalian agility and a handy prehistoric tree saved Quizkid.
Snarling Cynognathus must find other bones to crunch.

The Phytosaurs, cheated of their prey, fight over the hapless Eupelor.

TERATOSAURUS, the fierce Triassic carnivore, contemplates a meal. His sluggish reptilian circulation is quickened by the growing warmth of the sun, and he's ready to pounce.

From the safety of a giant conifer Quizkid looks out over the sun-dappled uplands. His heart beats fast with excitement but his steady eye misses no detail of the browsing herds.

YALEOSAURUS and PLATEOSAURUS are herbivorous dinosaurs, so Quizkid has nothing to fear from these mild-eyed ungainly creatures.

But Coelophysis, the cannibalistic carnivore, is another matter. The saw-toothed predator is about to gulp down a luckless juvenile of his own species. Storm clouds are gathering; fire from the sky may strike the trees. Best to go back to the Present.

Notebook

● The first dinosaurs appeared in the Triassic Period (Try-ASS-ic). That is, the earliest remains of dinosaurs have been found in rocks belonging to that period.

● The Triassic Period began about 240 million years ago and lasted about 40 million years. We say 'about' because in dealing with these enormous periods of time it is not possible to be accurate to the century.

● The first primitive men appeared about 3 million years ago.

● About 150 years ago mammals of the species *Homo sapiens* (man) examined the fossil bones and teeth of unknown animals and decided, correctly, that they were the remains of giant extinct reptiles.

● The name DINOSAURIA (DIE-no-SAU-ria) was suggested for these reptiles. 'Dinosaur' comes from two Greek words meaning 'terrible' and 'lizard'. The Dinosaurs, however, were not lizards, and they were not all terrible.

Classification

There were two main kinds of dinosaur, and they are classified on the basis of the shape of their hip bones.

One group, the SAURISCHIA (Sau-RISK-ia), have pelvic bones like those shown in Diagram A on the facing page. Saurischia means 'lizard hips'.

Reptiles and other land animals have three kinds of bone at the point

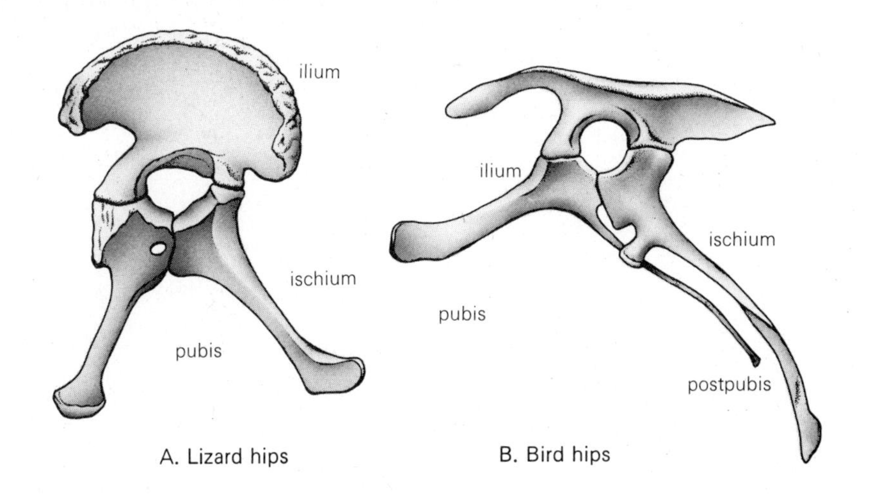

A. Lizard hips

B. Bird hips

where their hind legs meet their spine: the *ilium*, which is joined to the backbone; the *pubis*, in front, and the *ischium* (ISK-ium), behind. In Saurischian dinosaurs these three bones are arranged as in Diagram A: you can see how they come off the leg-bone socket.

The other group, the ORNITHISCHIA (Orni-THISK-ia), have pelvic bones like those shown above on the right. Ornithischia means 'bird hips'.

In Ornithischian dinosaurs there are four bones coming off the leg-bone socket; as you can see from Diagram B, the pubic bone has two parts; one goes back and one goes forward. The forward bone supports the belly. Birds have pelvic bones something like this, but birds are not descended from Ornithischian dinosaurs though birds and Ornithischian dinosaurs had an ancestor in common far back in time.

There are two kinds of Saurischian dinosaurs:

1. THEROPODS (THEER-opods) – carnivores
2. SAUROPODS (SAU-ropods) – amphibious herbivores

There are four kinds of Ornithischian dinosaurs:

1. ORNITHOPODS (orn-ITH-o-pods)
2. STEGOSAURS (STEGG-o-saurs)
3. ANKYLOSAURS (an-KYE-lo-saurs)
4. CERATOPSIANS (serra-TOPS-ians)

These were all herbivores. Herbivores eat plants; carnivores eat meat. Amphibious means they could live in water as well as on land.

All Saurischian and Ornithischian dinosaurs were reptiles, and all of

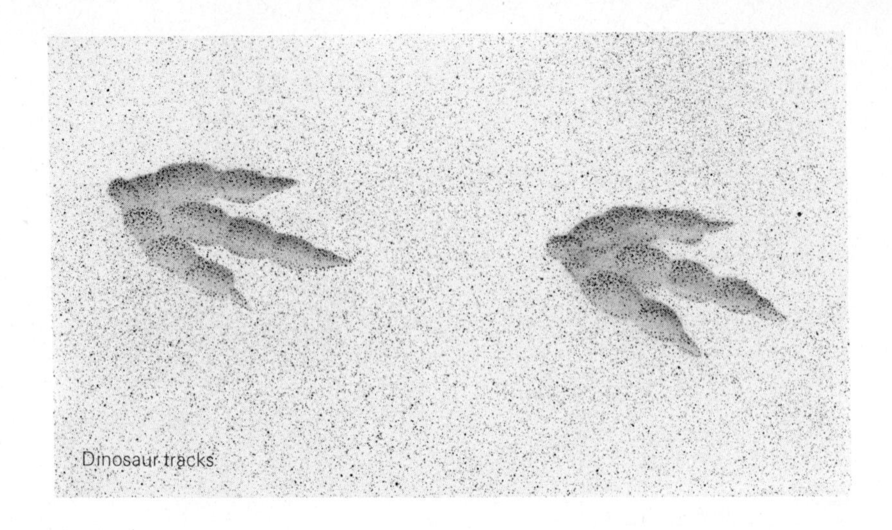
Dinosaur tracks

them (as far as we know) laid eggs ; they buried their eggs in the ground and left them to hatch. When the young dinosaurs hatched they were on their own. Their parents did not feed them or teach them to hunt ; on the contrary, some dinosaurs ate their young.

Dinosaur Senses

Dinosaurs could see, and hear, and smell, and no doubt made noises. But they had very small brains and were certainly stupid. Their eyes and ears and noses told them 'food', or 'danger', or 'too hot', 'too cold', or 'opposite sex'. But these messages would travel very slowly from brains to legs. They were probably, therefore, slow to get moving ; and after a burst of energy, they had to rest. Watching dinosaurs would have been like watching a slow-motion film. Plenty of time for an active, quick-thinking, more intelligent mammal to get out of the way.

Reptilian Characteristics

All reptiles are 'cold-blooded'. They need heat to warm up their blood and make them active. If it is chilly, they are torpid. If it is too hot, they have to find somewhere to cool off.

Dinosaurs probably had scaly, or leathery, or horny skins. These

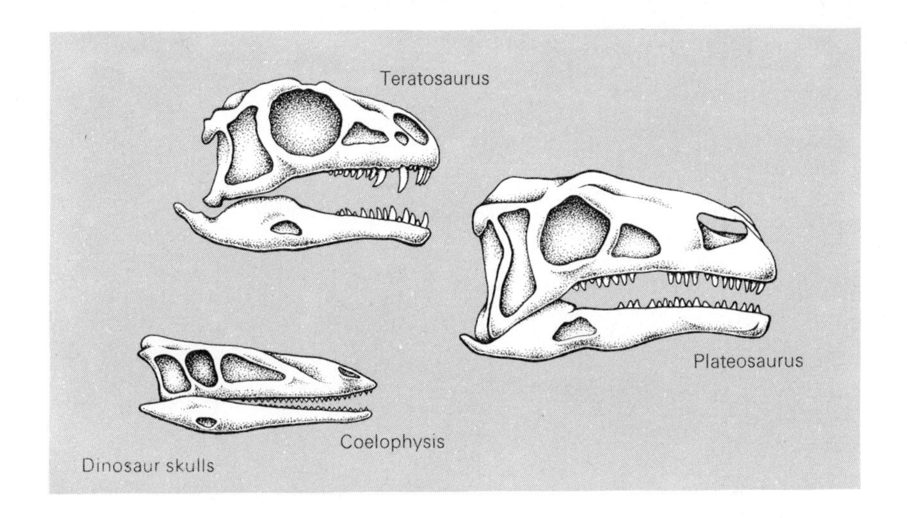

Dinosaur skulls

allowed the sun to warm their blood. We do not know whether these skins were coloured. Some modern reptiles, snakes and lizards, for example, are brightly coloured and prettily patterned. Perhaps the dinosaurs were too. During the Mesozoic Era (MESS-o-ZO-ic) climates were warm, so the dinosaurs flourished. They flourished for 130 million years. Will man flourish so long and so successfully?

Triassic Fauna (Animal Life)

PHYTOSAURS (FI-to-SAURS): Not crocodiles, but modern crocodiles are like them. They were ferocious carnivores, extinct at the end of the Triassic Period.

CYNOGNATHUS (SIGH-no-GNATHUS – 'a' as in hath), a mammal-like reptile, looked like a dog-lizard or a lizard-dog. They had three kinds of teeth, grinders, piercers and biters (other reptiles had only one kind). They had better breathing arrangements than the other reptiles and could breathe and eat at the same time. (Dinosaurs had no palate to separate their air passages from their food passages and had to gulp, breathe, gulp, breathe . . .) Cynognathus had legs with 'elbows' back, 'knees' forward, and could probably move quite fast. (Reptiles are sprawlers.) Perhaps Cynognathus had warm blood and a hairy coat, and perhaps females gave birth to live young and suckled them. These are all the characteristics of mammals. (Why would a hairy coat go with warm

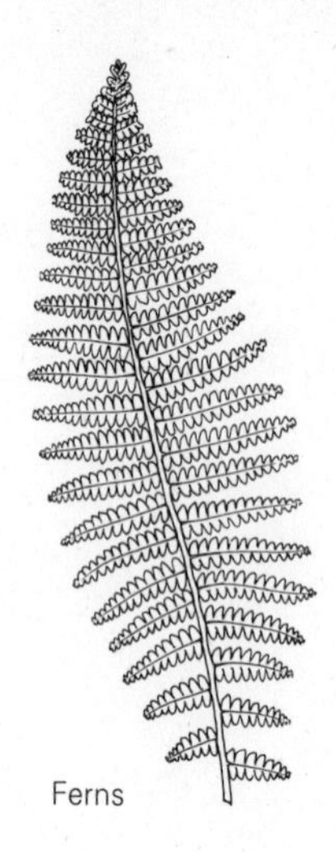
Ferns

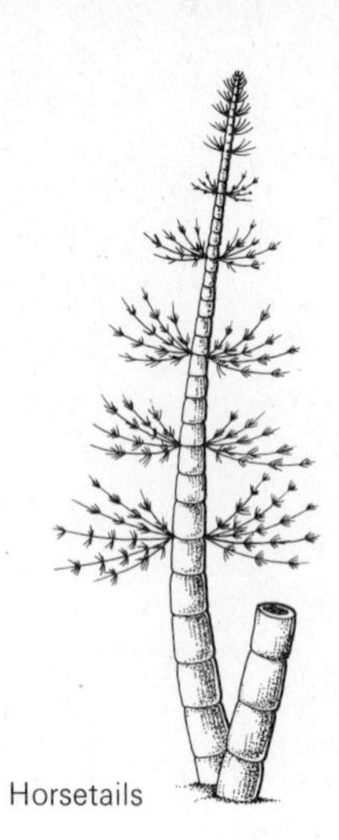
Horsetails

blood?) Cynognathus was extinct at the end of the Triassic Period, but a forerunner of things to come. This wasn't the 'beginning' of mammals; evolution is a process of infinitely slow change and you cannot pinpoint exactly when anything 'began'; but there were reptiles which were beginning to be mammal-like long before the Triassic Period.

TERATOSAURUS (TERRA-to-saurus): Bipedal (walked on its hind legs) theropod. Slow moving with heavy feet and solid bones, sharp teeth and claws. From Europe.

COELOPHYSIS (SEEL-o-phye-sis): Theropod. Smallish, about 2·4 metres (8 feet) long. Bones thin, leg bones hollow (like ours), seemingly 'built for speed'. Bipedal. Four-fingered 'hands' with sharp claws. Serrated teeth. In Mexico skeletons have been found with the bones of juveniles inside them (so we can assume that some of them were cannibalistic).

YALEOSAURUS (YALE-io-saurus): Prosauropod. Bipedal, but beginning to return to walking on four feet like its amphibian ancestors. This was probably because they were developing into bulky creatures who didn't have to chase their food. If they had to run from a predator they probably used their hind legs. Named after Yale, in America.

PLATEOSAURUS (PLATT-io-saurus): Prosauropod. Bipedal and quadrupedal, like Yaleosaurus. Six or more metres (20 feet or more) long, blunt teeth. From Europe.

EUPELOR (U-PEL-OR): Amphibian.

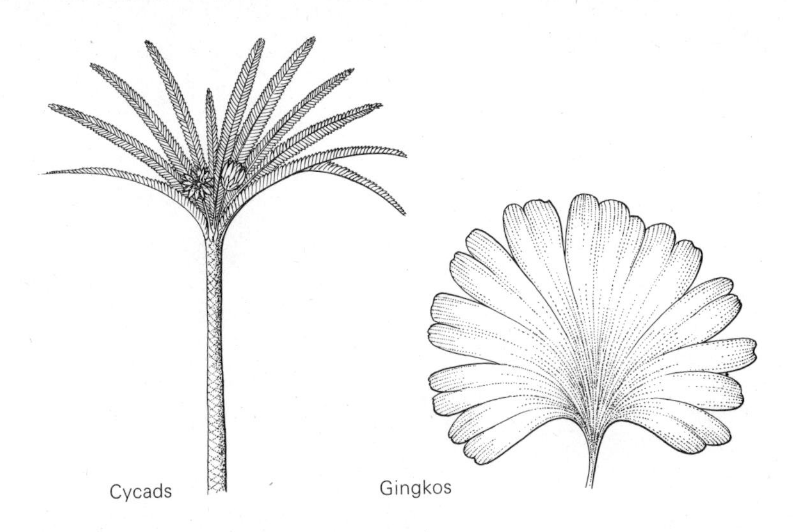

Cycads Gingkos

Triassic Flora (Plant Life)

Triassic trees were all conifers. Some of them were the forerunners of our 'monkey-puzzle' trees. In the forests there were also cycads, which had short palm-tree-like trunks with fronds on top; tree ferns, other kinds of fern, mosses and lichens. In the swamps grew horsetails with hollow rush-like stems. Descendants of the horse-tails and cycads can be found today; they are very ancient plants indeed. Triassic botanists (had there been any) wouldn't have had much to learn; there were only about 400 different kinds of plant. Angiosperms, or flowering plants, did not become widespread until the Cretaceous, and then their development was as rapid as the dinosaurs' had been.

The next great Period was the Jurassic (Ju-RASS-ic). What changes will Evolution have wrought? Quizkid, bright-eyed and cool-headed, sets the dial of his timepiece to Jurassic and once more leaves the Present for the Past.

Into the Jurassic

Splashdown took place in a Jurassic lake, but nothing daunted, the resourceful Quizkid surveys the scene from a convenient vantage-point. A BRONTOSAURUS is his unwitting steed.

RHAMPHORHYNCHUS swoops to investigate. Its teeth and claws are cruel. But the visitor to the past has brought a weapon from the future.
BRACHIOSAURUS
CETIOSAURUS
DIPLODOCUS
Time and evolutionary change have done their slow work. Gone are the Triassic prosauropods; now these colossal creatures, DIPLODOCUS, CETIOSAURUS, BRACHIOSAURUS, CAMARASAURUS, roam the land, surge and plunge in the tropical swamps, tear and gulp at the abundant vegetation.

The Brontosaurus has come ashore and is laying eggs, oblivious of the danger. Quizkid is doing his best to shift her, but can he prevent the tragedy ? 'This is Mother Nature's law,' he mutters to himself. 'Carnivore eats herbivore.'

ARCHAEOPTERYX, an early kind of
bird, has evolved its own means of escape
from the hunters.
ALLOSAURUS, the dreaded predator, is on
the hunt. Time for Quizkid to leave
Brontosaurus and save himself.

Quizkid, powerless to save the obliging Brontosaurus, has left the lakeside. Now, every sense alert, he explores the Jurassic jungle.
These harmless Camptosaurs, present no threat.
Compsognathus, although he is a theropod, is also harmless. His next meal is an early kind of cockroach.

STEGOSAURUS has developed formidable armour, but will it save him when he confronts the ferocious **MEGALOSAURUS**? Time is ticking away; Quizkid will be back in the Present before this conflict is resolved.
Another mammal-like reptile, **OLIGOKYPHUS**, leads a hunted life. **ORNITHOLESTES** has hands to grasp its prey, long legs to chase it.

Notebook

- The Jurassic Period began about 200 million years ago and lasted for 65 million years.
- In this period and the next, there were more dinosaurs than any other kind of animal.
- They were the dominant fauna ; they ruled the world.
- Some of them had evolved into giants.
- The sauropods were as big as land animals could possibly be. They had legs like pillars, spinal cords like cables, great padded feet, and kitten-sized brains.
- Fossilized sauropod footprints have been found in Texas. Each hind-footprint holds 68 litres of water, which is more than the average bath holds.
- The sauropods had small jaws and weak teeth. But there was plenty of lush food for them in the Jurassic.
- Their enemies were the giant carnivores.
- The carnivores had no enemies, only victims.
- There were many harmless Ornithischians in the Jurassic, and also much smaller mammal-like reptiles, and some mammals. These led a prudent life in the undergrowth. Probably they were nocturnal, coming out at night when the temperatures were lower and the dinosaurs slept.

Jurassic Fauna

BRONTOSAURUS (BRONT-o-SAUR-us), CAMARASAURUS (CAM-are-a-saurus), and DIPLODOCUS (Di-PLOD-ocus), all come from America, CETIOSAURUS (SEE-tio-SAU-rus) from England, and BRACHIOSAURUS (BRAKE-io-SAU-rus) from Africa. They are all examples of giant amphibious sauropods. There are two schools of thought among palaeontologists (PAL-i-ont-olo-jists – people who work with fossils) about these sauropods. One group says that the animals were adapted for a mainly aquatic life because they needed to take the weight off their feet (they weighed 30 tonnes or more). Water would have supported their unwieldy bodies and their teeth seem suitable for browsing on waterweeds, i.e. they were blunt and rather feeble. The other group, having worked out possible weights, says that the sauropods could have been land-living animals who only went into the water to bathe and splash themselves (as elephants do) and to escape predators. Since no one really knows for certain (shall we ever know?) you can believe whichever group you like. Diplodocus is the longest dinosaur so far discovered and had nostrils on top of its head (another argument for believing it spent most of its time in water): Brachiosaurus is the tallest, and was 12 metres (40 feet) high, or almost as high as three double-decker buses standing one on top of the other. Its front legs were longer than its back legs, making it rather giraffe-shaped. Its nostrils, too, were high on the skull.

Oligokyphus

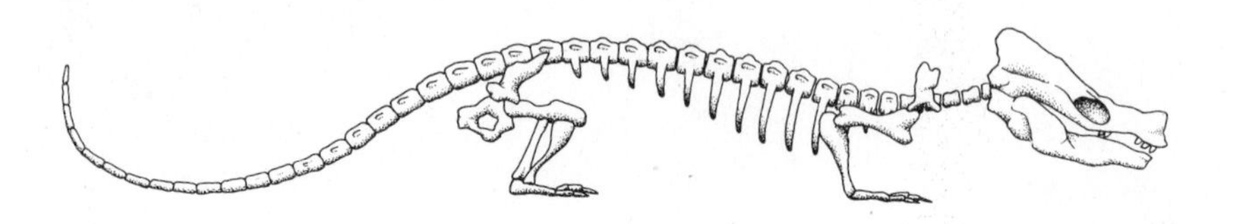

ALLOSAURUS, also called ANTRODEMUS, and MEGALOSAURUS (AL-o-saurus, AN-tro-deem-us, MEG-al-o-saurus): Giant therapods; the same basic design as the Triassic Teratosaurus, but bigger. About 9 metres (30 feet) long. Solid bones, but had an expandable skull for swallowing chunks of flesh. Sharp claws. Bipedal. Megalosaurus was the first dinosaur to be discovered and described in England; Allosaurus comes from America.

CAMPTOSAURUS (CAMP-toe-saurus): An ornithopod 4 metres (15 feet) long. Both bipedal and quadrupedal. Spike-like thumb. America.

COMPSOGNATHUS (COMP-so-GNATHUS): A small theropod, about 608 millimetres (2 feet) long, head 76 millimetres (3 inches) long. Europe.

ORNITHOLESTES (orni-tho-LEST-eez): A therapod, much the same basic design as the Triassic Coelophysis. Name means 'bird-catcher' but it probably lived on small animals. America.

OLIGOKYPHUS (OLLY-go-KYE-fuss): A mammal-like reptile about the size of a rabbit with a long body and short legs; probably covered in fur, and the female had milk-glands. Probably lived in colonies. From England.

STEGOSAURUS (STEGG-o-saurus): An 'armour-plated' dinosaur, 6 metres (20 feet) long. High hips, low front legs, spiked tail. The purpose of the double row of vertical plates on the spine is unknown. Famous for its 'second-brain'—really an enlarged nerve centre in the pelvic region

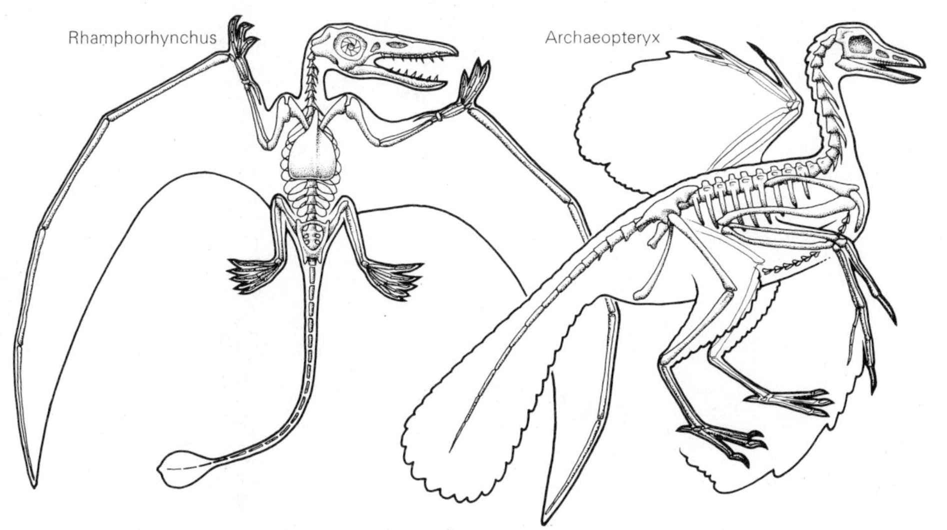

which relayed messages from the head. Many other dinosaurs had these nerve centres. America.

RHAMPHORHYNCHUS (RAM-fo-RING-kuss) : A pterosaur or flying reptile, with 590 millimetre (2 foot) wing span, long pointed teeth, and a tail. It had three hook-like fingers, perhaps for hanging by when roosting.

Jurassic Flora

Times were good for herbivores in the Jurassic. The world was still decorated with the browns and greens of conifers, gingkos (the Maiden-hair tree, still to be found today), ferns, cycads, horsetails and mosses and lichens. But in the mild, warm, damp air, vegetation grew thick and green and juicy. Not only did it feed the dinosaurs, but the undergrowth provided shelter for insects, small reptiles, amphibian frogs and toads. Perhaps here and there flowering plants were beginning to evolve, but the most conspicuously coloured plants were probably the cycads with their flower-like cones.

Quizkid now sets the dial to the third and last period of the Mesozoic Era – the Cretaceous.

Into the Cretaceous

In the exciting Cretaceous surroundings Quizkid observes the varied Cretaceous fauna. The development of mountain ranges is a feature of the Cretaceous Period.

PACHYCEPHALOSAURUS was a bone-head. He had an extremely thick skull. What, Quizkid wonders, is the evolutionary value of this? No one knows.

Harmless **HYPSILOPHODON** cracks an early walnut.

Two **IGUANODONS**. They have eyes for no one but each other, this pair of romantic reptiles.

Dozens of different duckbills haunt this lake shore. The delighted Quizkid fills his notebook.

EDMONTOSAURUS, LAMBEOSAURUS, ANATOSAURUS, KRITOSAURUS, PARASAUROLOPHUS are all hadrosaurs. Why the duck-type bills?

Why have so many kinds of headcrest evolved? This is another evolutionary puzzle.

Peaceful herds of ceratopsians, **MONOCLONIUS, PENTACERATOPS, STYRACOSAURUS,** browse in the evening sunlight. It is difficult to realize that they were reptiles and laid eggs. Why are there more herbivores than carnivores?

Quizkid feeds these little mammals with early figs. He looks indulgently at them; they are his ancestors, but they have a long way to go.

ANKYLOSAURUS fears no foe, encased in his plated armour. His massive tail can swing like a club, but Quizkid knows he is a herbivore and harmless.

The eternal drama of carnivore and herbivore, hunter and hunted, predator and prey. Here the herbivore, TRICERATOPS, is getting the best of it; he is seeing off the formidable GORGOSAURUS.

A sinister shadow looms; Quizkid, for the last time, should beware!

At the terrible roar that fills the air, the mammals make for the undergrowth, the hadrosaurs head for the water, the ceratopsians lumber into the sheltering trees, Ankylosaurus cowers inside his armour plating. Only the dauntless Quizkid dares confront Tyrannosaurus rex, the Tyrant king. But he had better turn the dial of his geologic timepiece to Present, while there is still time!

The recumbent reptile has used up his energy and he is sluggish in the evening chill. Quizkid kept his head; he knew he could dodge the terrible predator. The moon and the evening stars are rising; earth may change but they are constant.

The reign of the reptiles is nearly over. Soon they will all go into the dark, and the sun will rise on a world without dinosaurs. Then the tiny bright-eyed mammals will at last come into their own. Quizkid, his journey ended, returns to the Present.

Notebook

● In the Cretaceous (Cret-AY-shus) Period, 135 million–65 million years ago, climates were warm at first, cooler towards the end.

● Shallow seas covered much of the world.

● Chalky sediments deposited by these seas built up the white cliffs of Dover.

● Movements of the earth's crust created great mountain ranges: the Rockies, and the Andes. This was called the Laramide Revolution.

● The flora changed; cherry, willow, poplar, walnut, fig and magnolia all flowered and bore fruit in Cretaceous forests.

● Never before had herbivorous dinosaurs flourished as they flourished then.

● Never in time had there been such a variety of reptiles.

● But when the Cretaceous Period closed, that was the end of the dinosaurs. They became extinct; they died out, and in a short period of time, geologically speaking. There is a break in the fossil record. In rocks of the late Cretaceous Period dinosaur bones have been found. Then there is a gap, a layer of rocks in which no such fossils exist; and in the layer above that, bones appear again, but they are not the bones of dinosaurs.

● What happened? Lots of people have made guesses. Radio-active rays from Outer Space? Infectious epidemic disease? The mammals ate up the dinosaur eggs? The glands which govern growth and size got out of control? The race of dinosaurs just grew old and died, as individuals

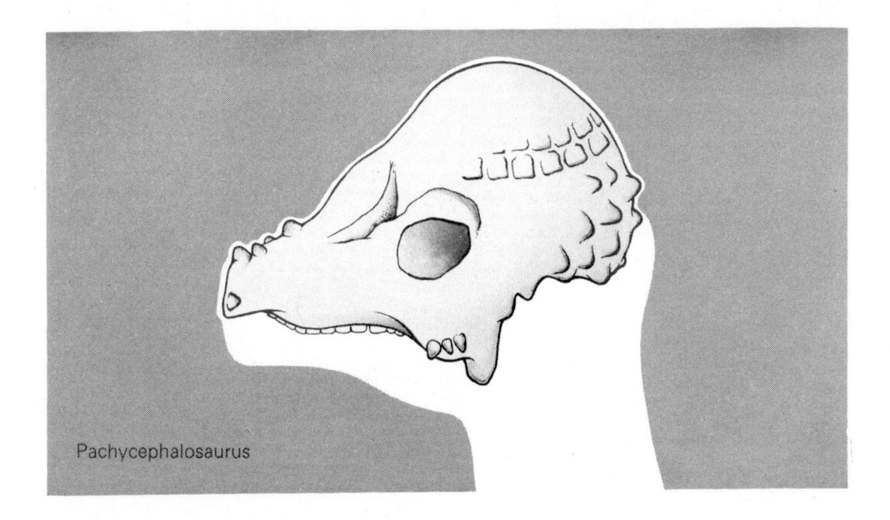
Pachycephalosaurus

do, and did not reproduce? The climate grew too cold? Too hot? Too wet? Too dry? The food supply changed or disappeared? Dinosaurs were just too stupid to live? Nobody knows for sure.

● Some reptiles persisted: crocodiles, alligators, turtles, tortoises, snakes and lizards including the tuatara of New Zealand, which has hardly changed since dinosaur days. Why did they survive? Flying reptiles and marine reptiles vanished too; but birds and fish are still with us.

● Why did it happen? The best guess is that probably the environment changed. Mountain ranges were thrown up, the seas ebbed and flowed; the climate changed with the environment and the dinosaurs were so specialized—the conditions under which they could survive were so limited—that they could not adapt, and so they perished.

● Then the mammals who had waited their turn for so long, 150 million years had room to spread and grow and change in turn, and did so.

● Will *Homo sapiens* become extinct? If so, what kind of animal may be waiting to take over from us?

Cretaceous Fauna

PACHYCEPHALOSAURUS (PACK-i-SEFF-a-lo-saurus): Means 'massive-headed reptile'. Ornithischian. Skull 254 millimetres (10 inches) thick. No complete skeleton has yet been found; a rare dinosaur, but who knows what bones still lie in the earth? Eastern America and West Asia.

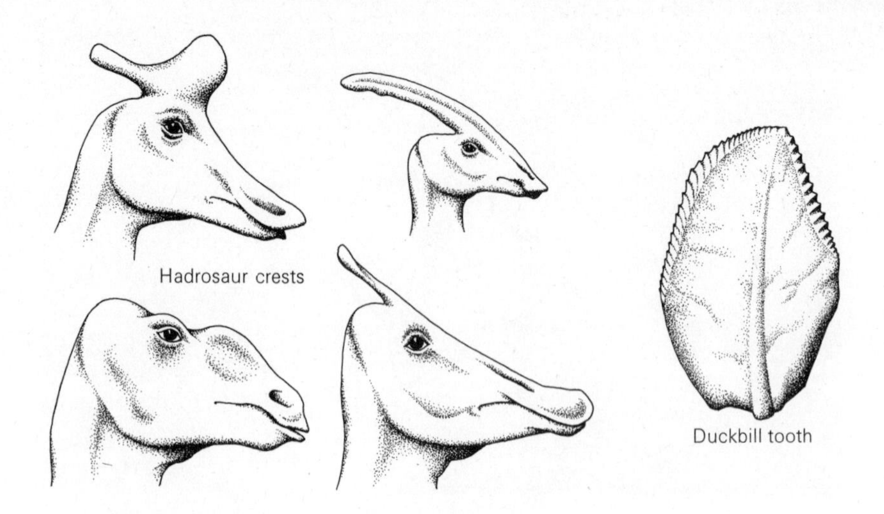

HYPSILOPHODON (HIPS-i-LOFF-o-don): A bipedal ornithopod. Small, about 1 metre (3+ feet). Rooster sized. Upper and lower jaws formed a beak. Feet probably able to grasp. Could probably run up branches. England.

IGUANODON (ig-WA-no-don): A bipedal Ornithischian, 6–9 metres (20–30 feet) long. Name means 'iguana tooth' because when fossils were found they were at first thought to be the remains of the giant lizard; but the reptile was not an iguana. Called the 'thumbs-up' dinosaur because of its spike-like thumbs. The second dinosaur to be found in England has left its footprints in Sussex, Dorset and the Isle of Wight. (The town of Maidstone in Kent, where bones were found in a quarry, has a dinosaur on its coat-of-arms.) Skeletons have also been found in Australia, North Africa, Europe, Mongolia. Many species are known.

HADROSAURS (HADD-ro-saurs): Ornithischians, the 'duck-bill' dinosaurs. Bipedal, but probably quadrupedal as well. Good swimmers; webbed feet, long strong tails. Remarkable teeth; up to 2,000. When the old teeth wore down, new ones took their place. Thousands of hadrosaurs have been found in America. Some like ANATOSAURUS (An-AH-to- saurus) had flat heads; others like KRITOSAURUS (KRYE-to-saurus) and PARASAUROLOPHUS (PARA-sauro-LOAF-us) had crests, some solid and some hollow. No one can be quite sure what purpose these crests served. Some palaeontologists think they were for holding a reserve air supply when the animal was feeding underwater. Others

Ankylosaurus

think they may have been 'resonance' chambers, for making bigger and better noises, but others think they provided an enlarged surface for stimulating the sense of smell, a useful anti-predator device. This is the most likely answer. It is always assumed that the hadrosaurs fed on rushes and water plants. But in the stomach of one Anatosaurus were found twigs, seeds, fruits and needles of evergreens. What were they doing there if he was a water feeder?

EDMONTOSAURUS (ed-MON-to-saurus): Apparently the largest hadrosaur, 12 metres (40 feet) long; we also have an impression of its fossilized skin; it looks rather like a crocodile skin.

TRICERATOPS (try-SERRA-tops): Ceratopsian. The bulkiest horned dinosaur. Quadrupedal. Horned dinosaurs had enormous heads, a varying number of horns, and a bony frill extending over neck and shoulders; this seems to suggest they met danger head-on. PENTACERATOPS (PEN-to-SERRA-tops) had five horns. MONOCLONIUS (MON-o-CLONE-ni-us) had one, STYRACOSAURUS (STYE-rack-o-saurus) had a straight thick nose-horn and spikes on its frill. *Styrax* is Greek for a group of resinous plants.

GORGOSAURUS (GOR-go-saurus): A giant therapod. 9 metres (30 feet) long. Feeble forelimbs and tiny two-fingered hands. From Mongolia.

ANKYLOSAURUS (An-KYE-lo-saurus): An armoured dinosaur, described as a ponderous animated citadel. Ornithischian. Bony armour

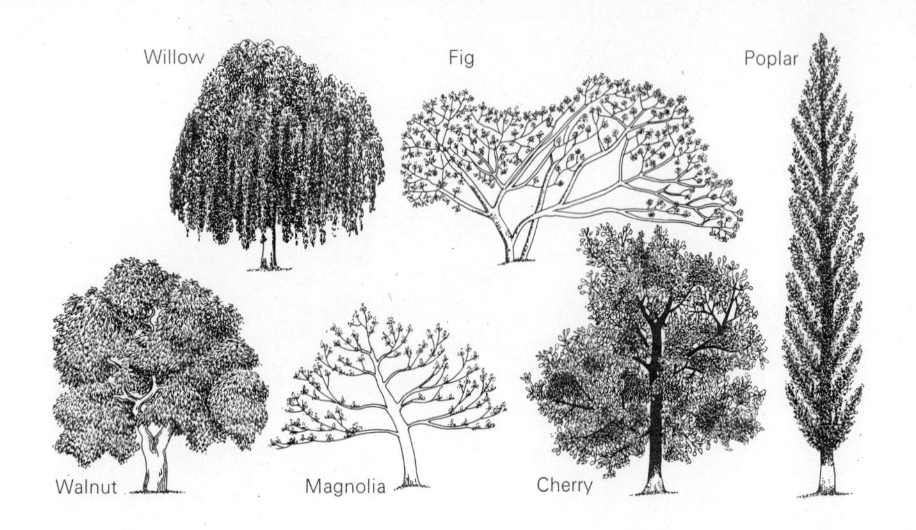

covered its whole body, and it had a tail like a massive club. It was well protected against predators. 5 metres (17 feet) long and 2 metres (5 feet) wide, it probably moved extremely slowly. America.

TYRANNOSAURUS REX (tie-RAN-o-SAUR-us): The largest and most formidable of all the giant carnivores. 15 metres (50 feet) long, skull 1 metre (4 feet) long. Teeth serrated, but rather blunt. Feeble forelimbs. America.

Cretaceous Flora

The Jurassic flora continued into the early Cretaceous, but then a rich change took place. There was a very rapid evolution of the angiosperms, the flowering plants. Today these outnumber all the other kinds of plants in the world, and man depends upon them for many things. The Middle Cretaceous has been described as 'the springtime of the world'. Along with buds, flowers, fruits, seeds, the birds and butterflies evolved and flourished. Some of the new trees were the deciduous ones we know today; magnolia, oak, walnut, willow, fig, cherry, poplar, elm, beech; and there were evergreens: ivy and laurel. The first autumns came to the world, too, with the fall of the leaves.